About the Book

Little Raccoon Baby was born in May, when the flowers were blooming and the springtime air was filled with the sweet sounds of chirping birds. She was grey and fuzzy and only three inches long.

Soon she was big enough to play with her brother and sister. They loved to climb all over each other, falling topsy-turvy in a furry heap. They were so soft and roly-poly that they didn't get hurt as they tumbled about.

But one day the raccoon family visited a country farm. Far off in the distance they thought they heard low rumbling sounds. All of a sudden, a great big growling dog came crashing through the trees, bounding toward them with his teeth bared! What would the baby raccoons do, and how could their mother protect them?

Berniece Freschet and Jim Arnosky have created a delightful book about a black-masked baby raccoon and her adventures exploring a brand new world with curiosity and spunk.

RACCOON BABY

by Berniece Freschet

pictures by Jim Arnosky

G.P. Putnam's Sons • New York

A See & Read Book

For Taryn, with special love

Text copyright © 1984 by Berniece Freschet
Illustrations copyright © 1984 by Jim Arnosky
All rights reserved. Published simultaneously in
Canada by General Publishing Co. Limited, Toronto.
Printed in the United States of America.
Library of Congress Cataloging in Publication Data
Freschet, Berniece.
Raccoon baby.
(A See & read book)
Summary: Describes the life of a baby raccoon from her birth
in May to the beginning of her first winter which she
spends in a cozy den with her mother and two siblings.
1. Raccoons—Juvenile literature. 2. Animals, Infancy of—Juvenile literature.
[1. Raccoons. 2. Animals—Infancy]
I. Arnosky, Jim, ill. II. Title. III. Series.
QL737.C26F73   1984   599.74′443   83-4634
ISBN 0-399-61149-5
First impression.

T 4026

CONTENTS

1 • A PLACE TO HIDE

It was May.

Green grass pushed up.

Leaf buds opened.

The air was sweet with the smell

of new growing things.

May was the month

when new babies were born.

A raccoon looked for a den.

A quiet, secret place,

high up, away from leaping dogs.

And hidden away from people.

The raccoon found her den
inside a hollow tree.
It was small and cozy,
lined with soft dry leaves.
Early the next day,
three baby cubs were born.
They were tiny—
only three inches long.
Their eyes were shut tight.
They could not see or hear.
They were covered with grey fuzz
and looked as if they wore
black masks over their eyes.

The mother raccoon
licked her new babies,
one after the other,
over and over again.
She pulled them
close to her warm body.
The newborn cubs were hungry.
They found their mother's nipples
and drank her warm milk.
When their stomachs were full,
they went to sleep.
The mother raccoon did not
leave her den even to eat.

But on the third day
she was very hungry.
She climbed down the tree
and found some dry seeds
and berries by a stream.
Before eating the food,
she swished it in the water,
which raccoons often do
if water is nearby.

After digging in the sand,

the mother raccoon found

some turtle eggs.

She ate them and felt stronger.

Then she sat down and cleaned herself.

An owl hooted.

"Whooo—Whoooo!"

The raccoon listened.

Did the sound come
from near her den?
An owl was a danger
to her young.
"Whooo—Whoooo!"
The mother raccoon
rushed back to her
helpless, newborn babies.

2 • A LONG WAY DOWN

Most of the time the baby
raccoons ate and slept.
Day by day, they grew bigger.
In three weeks
their eyes opened.
Soon they could hear.
Their fur grew long.
Now their tails had the same
black rings as their mother's.
The little raccoons stood.
They made twittering sounds,
and crawled topsy-turvy
over each other.

As they grew strong,

they began to climb.

They wanted to get outside.

But they did not get far

before they fell back into the nest.

They were not strong enough

to climb all the way up the tree

to the opening.

But Raccoon Baby kept trying.

The mother raccoon went

looking for food.

But she did not go far

nor stay away too long.

When she returned, the babies made
soft chirring sounds.
The mother kept a careful watch
for enemies: the skunk and the bobcat,
the owl and the fox.
No animal came near the den
when the mother was close.
She was a fierce fighter.
One day Raccoon Baby climbed
all the way up the tree.
She peeked out the opening
and blinked.

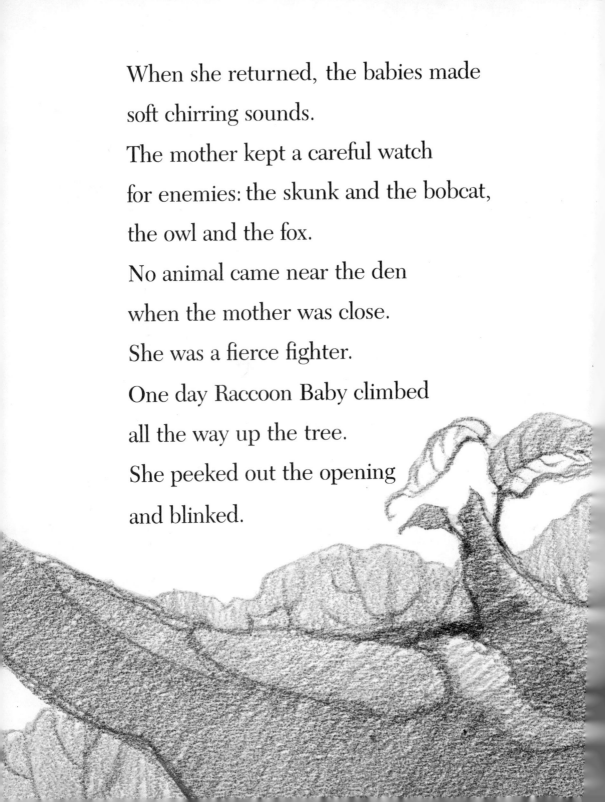

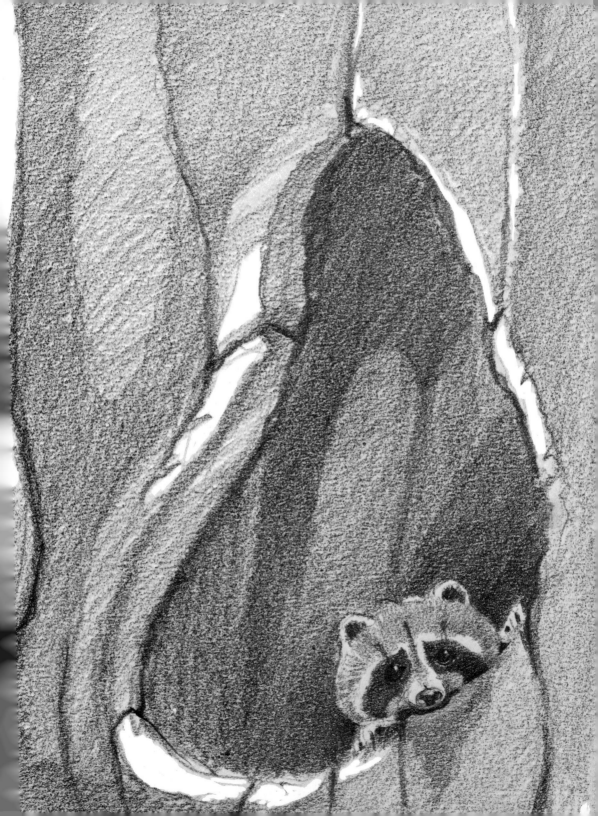

How bright it was.

She heard the rustle of leaves

and the call of a crow.

"Caw—caw—caw!"

Raccoon Baby pushed outside the hole.

The ground was far below.

Suddenly, a grey squirrel jumped near.

Leaves brushed Raccoon Baby's fur.

She began to shake.

She lost her grip

and down she fell!

Raccoon Baby was not hurt
when she landed.
For the ground was soft
with the new grass.
But she was afraid.
She cried for her mother.
Quickly, her mother ran to her.
She picked up Raccoon Baby
and carried her up the tree,
back to the safe, warm den.

The baby raccoons spent
most of their time playing.
They tumbled over each other,
nipping on ears and noses.
They climbed on their mother's back
and nibbled on her tail.
When they were six weeks old,
all the cubs were able to climb up
to the opening.
Raccoon Baby was the first
to push out onto a limb.
She hung on tight.
She would not fall again.

When they were two months old,
the mother raccoon coaxed her young
down the tree.
Slowly the baby raccoons
backed down, their small paws
clinging tightly to the bark.

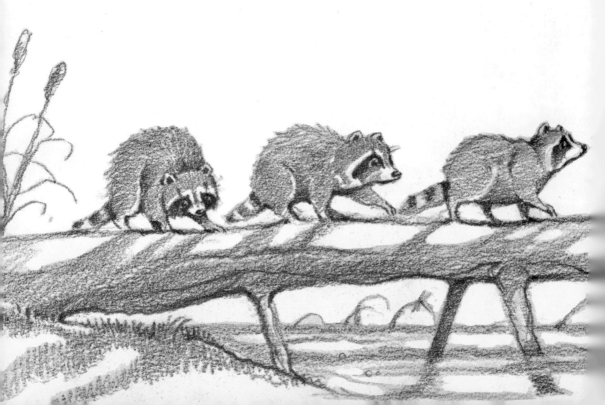

On wobbly legs
they followed their mother.
She took her young
down the path to the stream.
It was an exciting new adventure
for Raccoon Baby.

3 • RUN FOR YOUR LIFE

Raccoon Baby pushed her nose
under rocks and into holes
and hollow logs.
She was very curious.
Everything was new
and had to be explored.
Other animals were also out
hunting for food.
Raccoon Baby met a porcupine
who grunted at her.
Somehow she knew
to stay out of his way.

She saw a mother skunk
with her young, and a possum
with her babies
inside her pouch.
When they got to the stream,
the mother waded into the water.
She fished for tadpoles
as the young raccoons
watched from the bank.

They still drank only
their mother's milk.
But a few nights later
they were eating beetles and grubs.
Soon Raccoon Baby was fishing
in the stream beside her mother.
The raccoon family did not
go back to their den.
Now they slept in trees
and hollow logs by day.
At night they hunted for food.

Raccoon Baby ate whatever
she could find:
earthworms and bugs,
beetles and grubs,
snails and crayfish,
and small frogs
—when she could catch them.
Raccoon Baby and her brothers
liked to play in the water.

Soon they could swim.

The raccoons spent the summer

eating and playing and growing.

By fall they were almost
as big as their mother.
Now they ate all the time.
They needed a thick layer
of fat to get them through
the long, cold winter.
One night the mother
took her young to a farm.
She made sure no dogs were near.
A dog was a great danger.

The mother pushed over
a stock of corn and showed
her young how delicious
the yellow ears tasted.
There were also sweet, juicy apples,
and fresh eggs in the hen house.
That night the raccoons ate
so much they could hardly
waddle back to the woods.
They visited the farm often.

One night in the cornfield they heard
the barking of a dog close by.
Mother Raccoon chittered loudly.
Danger—run! Run!
The raccoons ran as fast
as their fat, round bodies could go.
There was a loud, thrashing noise.

In a sudden bound,

a large dog leaped out

of the cornfield after them!

They were almost to the woods.

The dog was right on their heels.

The mother raccoon would have

to fight to save her young.

She turned to face the enemy,

as the young raccoons

climbed to safety.

The big dog showed his sharp teeth.

Growling, he jumped forward!

The mother raccoon lashed

out with her sharp claws.

The dog gave a yelp of pain.

He rubbed his stinging nose

in the cool grass.

The mother raccoon quickly

ran to a tree and climbed up.

The raccoon family was safe.

In November the first snow fell.

Deep in the woods

the raccoons found a new den.

A quiet, hidden place,

away from blowing winds

and winter's deep snows.

Here they would stay until spring.

They curled up together—

a furry tail over each nose,

fat, round bodies

warming their cozy den.

A cold wind whistled
outside their tree.
The raccoons snuggled close.